Famous Children's Authors
Book II

By
Shirley Norby & Gregory Ryan

Publishers
T.S. Denison & Company, Inc.
Minneapolis, Minnesota 55431

DEDICATION

For all those who give back to the world in beauty and caring what they can, and for Richard whose compassionate heart and dedication to children makes this a better place for us all.

Shirley Norby

"For you."
Gregory Ryan

T.S. DENISON & CO., INC.

No part of this publication may be reproduced or transmitted by any means, mechanical or electronic, including photocopy, recording, or stored in any information storage or retrieval system without permission from the publisher.

Standard Book Number: 513-01956-1
Famous Children's Authors, Book II
Copyright © 1989 by T.S. Denison & Co., Inc.
Minneapolis, Minnesota 55431

Introduction for the Children

Pippi, Corduroy, Frederick, and Peter Rabbit are some of the well-known story characters created by the authors and illustrators you will read about in this book. We selected these twenty people because they are popular with our students, their books are outstanding, and they are favorites of ours. In the case of Carolyn Keene, she is a bit of a mystery herself, as you probably know if you have ever tried to locate information about her for a book report!

We work together in a small New Jersey elementary school near the Atlantic Ocean. As a teacher and a librarian, we have been bringing children and books together for over forty years. We have shared story books, joke books, poetry books, books about monsters, athletes, and folk heroes. For a long time we looked for a book about authors and illustrators, but we could not find one that was just right for our students. So we decided to write one called *Famous Children's Authors.* That proved to be so popular that we were asked to write a sequel which is the one you are reading now. We hope that our readers will like this one as well so we can keep writing more books about authors for young readers.

We started by reading library books and magazine articles about these men and women. We also wrote letters to them, if they were still alive, asking questions about their childhood experiences, families, school memories, pets, and things that were not found in the library. Many of them wrote back to us with their answers. We put all the information together and wrote it down to share with you. We had great fun writing this book and we hope you and your friends will have fun reading it. Each author story is followed by a list of their book titles, so you will know what to ask for when you go to the library. Some of the books you will be able to enjoy now. Others you may have to read when you are a little older.

As you read this book, you will be interested to find out that many of these writers decided when they were very young that they would like to create stories or pictures when they were all grown-up. Have **you** ever thought that perhaps you would like to be an author or illustrator when you grow up? The best way to prepare is to start right now by reading, reading, reading! Also, you can get started by writing stories on your own. Share them with your teacher or family. Illustrate your own stories or ask a friend to illustrate them for you. Make a book of your own stories and give it as a gift to someone special. As soon as you finish one project, get started on another one.

Perhaps one day you will write or illustrate a book which millions of people will enjoy and they will read about **you** in a book of *Famous Children's Authors.*

A Message to Teachers and Librarians

• Organize a book event around the theme, "I Love Books." If this is done in February, students could write a Valentine to their favorite book character or design a Valentine that their favorite book character might send to a fictional or real person.

• Have a birthday party with simple refreshments and entertainment for a favorite author, past or present. Author need not be present to be honored.

• Make paper bag masks of favorite book characters and visit another classroom and the library. Have students and teachers guess who the masks represent.

• Have parents share favorite books that they remember enjoying as children.

• Have students write a different ending to a well-known fairy tale.

• Use wallpaper samples and lots of imagination to create animal stories in the style of Leo Lionni.

• Have a poetry day at least once a month in your classroom or library.

• Have students make shape books in the form of animals, letters, machines, etc.

• Using Indian legends like those in Paul Goble's stories, have students set the songs that are in these books to music by using rattles, drums, flutes, and whistles. Some students might want to make simple rattles out of stones or gourds. Others may want to use traditional rhythm instruments.

• Organize a meal or food festival around a theme, location, culture, title, or book character. Examples might be Indians, Nancy Drew books, Mother Goose rhymes, etc.

• Encourage students to write picture-letters like Beatrix Potter did. Stories could be written in code if desired.

• Write a sequel to a story. Good ones to use are *The Girl Who Loved Wild Horses* by Paul Goble or *Shoeshine Girl* and *White Bird* written by Clyde Robert Bulla. Sequels or different endings to these stories require thought provoking judgments on the reader's part.

• Design short and simple book slogans for bumper stickers, bulletin board boarders and bookmarks.

• Have students in the middle grades write classified lost and found ads revolving around the plot or character in a book recently read.

• Using pins and yarn, have students chart the settings of stories the class reads on a large map of the United States or the World. An alternate to charting story settings would be to chart the journeys that book characters make.

• Hold a reading raffle once a month. Prizes could be paperback books or a gift certificate to a fast food restaurant or ice cream store. The more the students read, the more raffle tickets they earn for each monthly drawing.

• Encourage students to write their own myths.

• Borrow a book of plays adapted from famous children's books and let your students be the performers. If time permits they could write their own play adaptations.

• Purchase or borrow spin-off books such as *The Peter Rabbit Craft Book* by Debbie Smith (Warne, $7.95) and saturate your class with activities related to a particular author's work.

• After you have shared a biographical sketch with your class, make a collection of that author's books available on your classroom reading shelf. Reading partners can share the books and plan projects together.

• Keep an eye out for new books by these authors as they become available. Your students will scramble to be the first to read these hot-off-the-press books as they arrive at your school.

CONTENTS

ALIKI

*"I like books.
I like the way a book feels.
I like the way a book smells."*

These are the opening sentences of Aliki's story of *How A Book Is Made.* They tell how she feels about books. Aliki has felt this way since her very first visit to a library when she was three or four years old. Two of her aunts, taking her by the hand, led her up the steps of the Camden, New Jersey Public Library and into a dimly lit, wood-filled room containing that special smell of books. Her aunts sat with her at a small table and read a book to her. She remembered this wonderful day when she wrote and illustrated *How A Book Is Made.* The first page shows a cat, without an aunt at each side, at a small desk turning the pages of a book and saying, *"I like books. I like the way a book feels. I like the way a book smells. I like to turn each page, read each word, look at the pictures."*

Aliki's full name is Aliki Liacouras Brandenberg but she only uses her first name when she writes and illustrates books. Her unusual name is Greek. She was born in New Jersey where her parents were vacationing but grew up in the Philadelphia, Pennsylvania area. Aliki, being Greek American with an unusual name always felt different. She never liked the way she looked but she knew she loved drawing. She decided to work hard at being good at what she could do well, instead of worrying about how she looked. Her teachers encouraged her "differentness" and her art. She remembers her Kindergarten and First Grade teachers exhibiting and praising her paintings and giving her art books to read. Aliki was always drawing in school, even when she was supposed to be doing something else. Her interest in words and writing began in the third grade when she was "bitten" by the vocabulary and English grammar bug. All through her school years she took Saturday art classes and after graduation attended the Philadelphia Museum College of Art.

She finished art school in 1951 and went to New York to work for a year in the display department of the J.C. Penney Company. Then she moved back to Philadelphia where she worked as a freelance artist painting murals, teaching ceramics and art, designing her own greeting cards and doing more work in display and advertising. She has always loved to work with her hands on creative and different art projects.

After working for five years Aliki decided to travel. She went to Italy and Greece to sketch and paint and visit the country where her parents had been born. Aliki speaks Greek and on this trip she learned a great deal about her Greek heritage. She also met the man whom she would later marry. His name was Franz Brandenberg and he is also a famous children's author!

Following their marriage, Franz and Aliki Brandenberg lived in Switzerland and later moved to New York where Aliki was asked to illustrate a "Let's Read and Find Out" science book. While working on it, an idea for another book popped into her head. This was *My Five Senses,* another Let's Read and Find Out book for young readers. She wrote *My Five Senses* in just a few days and went on to do many more books in this series published by the Thomas Y. Crowell Company.

Sometimes Aliki illustrates and other times she is both the author and illustrator. Aliki has illustrated more books than she has written. She and her husband, Franz, often work together as a team; he writes the stories and she draws the pictures.

Aliki and Franz presently live in London, England with their pet cat Nefertiti. Their two children, Jason and Alexa are grown-up. Aliki goes to her studio located on the top floor of her house every day to work. The studio is a quiet place, overlooking the gardens below. She works there alone for at least twelve hours (and sometimes longer) each day. She loves to work and says it is like breathing, a necessity to life. She doesn't have much leisure time, but when she does she loves reading, visiting her family and friends, working in her garden, cooking, and going to the theater and movies. She also likes to play baseball, watch tennis and travel. Her favorite places are in the mountains or by the ocean.

Aliki loves children and visits schools when she can. It makes her very happy to see that her books are read, loved and used. Aliki finds most children open to new ideas, curious, and alive with enthusiasm. She loves to talk to them and says that "**an unspoiled, honest child is a treasure.**"

When Aliki was a child, her favorite book was *Peter Rabbit.* She liked it because there were three girls and a boy in Peter's family just like hers. When asked if she had a favorite among those books she has published, she says that her books are like children; she loves each one as it is born within her soul. It gives her great pleasure to know that children and adults find her work worthwhile.

Selected Books Written and Illustrated by Aliki

How A Book Is Made
Keep Your Mouth Closed, Dear
The Wish Workers
Mummies Made In Egypt
A Medieval Feast
Go Tell Aunt Rhody
The Story of Johnny Appleseed
June 7
Three Gold Pieces
My Five Senses
A Weed Is A Flower: The Life of George Washington Carver
Hush Little Baby
My Visit to the Dinosaurs
The Eggs: A Greek Folktale Retold
The Two of Them
Feelings
Fossils Tell of Long Ago
Dinosaurs are Different
Diogenes; The Story of the Greek Philosopher
Digging Up Dinosaurs
Corn Is Maize: The Gift of the Indians
George and the Cherry Tree

CLYDE ROBERT BULLA

By the time he was seven, Clyde Robert Bulla knew that he wanted to be a writer. He was living then on a farm near King City, Missouri with his parents, two older sisters and one older brother. No one in his family had ever been a writer and they did not want him to spend his time writing stories. Only after his chores were done was he allowed to write or read books for pleasure. He did read a lot as a child but not the usual children's books found in libraries today. He read books from his parent's library and a few classics like *Tom Sawyer* and *Swiss Family Robinson* that he found in the school library. When he was five, he was given three books that became the only books he owned until he was an adult. They were *Peter Rabbit, Mother Goose,* and an alphabet book.

Born in 1914, he attended a one-room country school for his first eight grades. It was in this school that he began writing stories and songs. He then went for one year to the King City, Missouri High School and completed the next three years of school by correspondence. He would receive his assignments by mail, work on them at home, and return them to his teachers. His family was very poor and after graduating from high school he did not go to college. He went to work instead, and in his free time wrote stories for magazines, three long novels for adults, and more poetry, plays, and songs.

While working for a newspaper in King City, a pen pal friend from Louisiana suggested that he try writing stories for children. He told her that he didn't think he could but she gave him an idea for a book that turned out to be *The Donkey Cart*. He wrote it at night after finishing his newspaper work. The publication of *The Donkey Cart* in 1946 was the beginning of his career as a children's author. Today he has written more than fifty books on many different subjects and is famous! He says that if it hadn't been for his pen pal he might never have tried to write stories for young people.

Clyde Robert Bulla's books are perfect for the middle grade readers. His stories for boys and girls in these grades are not too long, or too short, but are JUST RIGHT! They have chapters, are illustrated and have eighty pages or less. Many of his stories are about children who are having some kind of difficulty.

Sarah Ida in *Shoeshine Girl* has trouble getting along with her parents and is sent away for the summer where she finds life is very different. Adam's family in *Cardboard Crown* objects to his friendship with a girl whom they consider a troublemaker.

He also writes wonderful stories about friendship, secrets, haunted houses, monsters, Indians, and many kinds of animals. *Dexter,* a book about a trained circus pony who is left for dead and must struggle to survive a harsh winter on his own, is dedicated to another famous children's author, Sid Fleischman. *White Bird* tells the story of a lonely orphan boy in Tennessee who is raised by the man who found him floating down a river in a cradle. This man doesn't want to have anything to do with other people and the boy doesn't have any friends except animals and birds for many years. Something happens to make the boy leave his isolated home and the man who has been his only father and teacher. Will he ever return? How does the man feel about losing his adopted son? Your heart will be touched by this story.

This author likes to visit schools and does so quite often. Many children write letters to him and he tries to answer them all. Sometimes they give him suggestions or story ideas for new books.

Writing a book takes Mr. Bulla a long time. ***"The hardest part is the first sentence,"*** he says. He begins with an idea that interests him and then he spends time thinking about characters, outlining the story, and writing the first draft. He makes many changes before sending a manuscript off to a publisher. The actual writing may take several months.

He loves to travel and has visited many countries. His favorite way to travel is by freighter ship. He tries to visit a place before writing about it. His home is now Los Angeles, California.

One book Clyde Robert Bulla has written for very young children is called *Keep Running, Allen!* Bulla fans would like to suggest that he should *Keep Writing, Clyde!* We want you to know that your stories are wonderful. Please give us fifty more!

A Selection of Books by Clyde Robert Bulla

My Friend the Monster
Shoeshine Girl
Beast of Lor
The Cardboard Crown
Conquista
Dandelion Hill
Dexter
The Ghost of Windy Hill
Last Look
A Lion to Guard Us
The Poppy Seeds
Riding the Pony Express
The Sword in the Tree
A Wish at the Top
Open the Door and See All the People
John Billington, Friend of Squanto
Indian Hill
The Valentine Cat
Squanto, Friend of the Pilgrims
White Bird
Viking Adventure
Old Charlie
Eagle Feather
The Donkey Cart
The Ghost Town Treasure
The Chalk Box Kid
Daniel's Duck
Pocahontas and the Strangers
St. Valentine's Day
Lincoln's Birthday
Keep Running, Allen
Joseph the Dreamer

MATT CHRISTOPHER

"The thing that helped me most in becoming a writer
was just sticking to it."

Matthew F. Christopher was born in Bath, Pennsylvania. At the age of seven his family moved to Portland, New York. As he grew, his interest in sports grew, too. He loved baseball so much that he and his friends were satisfied playing with a broom handle for a bat and a tennis ball.

It is no surprise that one of Matt Christopher's clearest memories of when he was a young boy going to school has to do with sports. During lunchtime the children were playing a game of football together on the playground. Everything was fine until Matt ripped his pants. Not just a little tear. The pants ripped full length all the way down one whole side. He ran the entire two miles home so he could change into another pair. That was his most embarrassing moment in school.

As a teenager he was not only interested in sports, he also became very interested in writing. He loved to write stories, especially sports stories.

"I started writing stories when I was fourteen, won a short story contest when I was eighteen, sold a one-act play and a short detective story when I was twenty-four, and have been selling ever since." He has written over 300 short stories and articles and has written a comic strip series called *"Chuck White and His Friends."*

Making a living as a writer did not come easily for Matt Christopher. Through the years he worked at different jobs with typewriter and cash register companies. In the evening, after work, he played semi-professional baseball. But all the while, he continued to make time for writing. He wrote one detective story each week for nearly a whole year before he finally sold one to a magazine which published it. He received only $50.00 for the story, but it encouraged him to keep writing. He has been a fulltime writer since 1963.

When asked how his first book came to be written, Matt Christopher answers: *"After having published 70 or 80 short stories, I decided to write a book on something I was really familiar with: sports. The result was The Lucky Baseball Bat."* His favorite book of all the ones he has written is *The Quarterback Switch*. Read it to find out why.

Young readers will find many exciting stories in Mr. Christopher's books. In the middle of all the excitement the main characters often learn something about themselves - and so does the reader. In *Little Lefty*, Bill Bailey finds out that being smaller than the other players doesn't have to hold you back. Little people who practice hard and try their best can make the BIG PLAYS just like everybody else.

You don't have to like baseball to enjoy Matt Christopher's books. He has written books about football, swimming, basketball, track, hockey, and dirt-bike racing. And he knows exactly what he is writing about. *"I spent many mornings watching PeeWee Hockey League games, as well as college hockey, before writing my book, Wingman on Ice."*

When he was twenty-three Matt married his wife, Catherine. They have raised three sons and one daughter and now have seven grandchildren. Today he lives in Rocky Hill, South Carolina.

How does he find the time to write all these books? Mr. Christopher works at home in his study everyday from about 9 a.m. to 4 p.m. with a little time out for lunch. In the evening he loves to read, watch some television, or go to a movie. One of his hobbies is playing horseshoes.

When he visits schools to share his books with the children, what he enjoys most is *"the children's honesty, their interest, and their eagerness to learn."*

You have already found out Matt Christopher's most embarrassing football memory. One of his happiest memories is when he played on a "pick-up" team in 1938 against the famous New York Giants baseball team. It must have been a great day since he still remembers it after 50 years.

So many young readers will remember Matt Christopher's action-packed books even longer than that!

A Selection of Books by Matt Christopher

The Lucky Baseball Bat
Baseball Pals
Basketball Sparkplug
Little Lefty
Touchdown for Tommy
Break for the Basket
Baseball Flyhawk
Catcher with a Glass Arm
The Counterfeit Tackle
Miracle at the Plate
The Year Mom Won the Pennant
The Basket Counts
Catch the Pass!
Shortstop From Tokyo
Jackrabbit Goalie

The Fox Steals Home
Johnny Long Legs
Look Who's Playing First Base
Tough to Tackle
The Kid Who Only Hit Homers
Face-Off
Mystery Coach
Ice Magic
No Arm in Left Field
Jinx Glove
Front Court Hex
The Team That Stopped Moving
Glue Fingers
The Pigeon With the Tennis Elbow
The Submarine Pitch

Power Play
Football Fugitive
Johnny No Hit
Soccer Halfback
Diamond Champs
Dirt Bike Racer
The Twenty-One Mile Swim
The Dog That Stole Football Plays
Run, Billy, Run
Desperate Search
Stranded
Earthquake
Devil Pony
Tight End
The Dog that Pitched a No-Hitter

Reprinted with Permission.
The Year Mom Won The Pennant.
Written by Matt Christopher.
Illustrated by Foster Caddell. Page 135.
Copyright © 1968 by Matt Christopher.
Published by Little, Brown and Company.

SID FLEISCHMAN

When you sit down to write a story how do you do it? When Sid Fleischman started writing, as a grown-up, he worked very fast. He once wrote a long mystery novel in three weeks. But his way of writing has changed. Now he sits at a typewriter on a giant pinewood table and works very slowly, choosing and typing each word until he gets the whole page just the way he wants it. *"On some days I will only get one page of work finished; on other days, five or six."* he says. You can imagine that it takes a lot of imagining first, before he puts the idea on paper, so that he'll get it right the first time.

Sid Fleischman is best known for his tall tales and adventure books. You might say that his *McBroom* stories are the tallest of tall books. He has written ten *McBroom* books so far, with more on the way probably. Each time he finishes one, before too long another pops into his mind. *"I tell myself that each new McBroom tale is positively the last - until the next irresistible idea makes a liar of me."*

His son, Paul Fleischman who is also a writer, remembers that when he was a little boy his father would work in his study all day. Then his mother would call Paul and his two sisters, Jane and Anne, into the living room where their father would read to them the chapter he had written that day. They loved being the first audience for what would later become a famous book. Sometimes they even made suggestions about what should happen next in the story.

Sid Fleischman did not set out to be a writer. When he was in grammar school he wanted to *"turn himself into a magician."* Since he learned his magic tricks from books, he visited every library he could and read every magic book he could find. Then he would get out his cards and coins to practice the tricks he had read about and try them out on his sisters. When he was in high school he and a friend put together a two-hour magic show which they performed in different places during the summertime. It was called "Mr. Arthur Bull's Francisco Spook Show."

When Sid was nineteen he wrote down all his favorite tricks and sent them to a publisher. *"Presto-change-o!"* They were published! Years later, *Mr. Mysterious & Company,* his first children's book, came about when he decided to write a book that his own children would enjoy. Here is his explanation of how it came about:

"When my three children were quite young they didn't understand what I did for a living. Other fathers left home in the morning and returned at the end of the day. I was always around the house. I sat down one afternoon and decided to clear up the mystery and write a book just for them. I put them in the story, my wife, my dogs, various friends, and even myself. That was twenty-four books ago."

Since 1962 his books have received many honors and awards. In 1988 his latest book, *The Whipping Boy* which is not a picture book, was awarded the Newbery Gold Medal. It is a book that took ten years of thinking and writing before it was finished.

Today Sid Fleischman still does magic tricks with cards and coins when he visits schools, but mostly he is a magician with words. He says, *"The storyteller and the magician have a great deal in common."* The characters of his stories surprise the reader with tricks all their own.

In *McBroom's Zoo* everyone helps track down unusual critters after a tornado twists across their "wonderful one acre farm" taking away all their amazing top soil. People come from miles around - even a villain - to see a Sidehill Gouger, a Silver-Tailed Teakettle, a genuine Desert Vamooser, a whole flock of Galoopus Birds, and a rare Spitback Giascutus. You will have to read the book for yourself, though, to find out about the very most unusual-est critter of them all, the Prairie Hidebehind.

Sid Fleischman, we're sure you will agree, is simply a wizard with words.

A Selection of Books by Sid Fleischman

Mr. Mysterious & Company	Mr. Mysterious' Secrets of Magic
By The Great Hornspoon!	The Ghost on Saturday Night
The Ghost in the Noonday Sun	The Whipping Boy
McBroom Tells the Truth	McBroom Tells a Lie
Chancy and the Grand Rascal	Me and the Man on the Moon-Eyed Horse
McBroom and the Big Wind	McBroom and the Beanstalk
Longbeard the Wizard	Humbug Mountain
McBroom's Ear	The Hey Hey Man
Jingo Django	McBroom and the Great Race
McBroom's Zoo	McBroom's Almanac
The Wooden Cat Man	McBroom's Ghost
McBroom the Rainmaker	Case of the 264 Pound Burglar
The Scarebird	(Bloodhound Gang Series)

DON FREEMAN

Would you rather spend your life playing the trumpet in a jazz band or creating picture books for children? That's a choice that Don Freeman had to make, but the New York City subway system helped him to decide.

Don Freeman was born August 11, 1908 in San Diego, California. He had one older brother, Warren. When he was just a young boy his mother died. She knew that her husband worked so much that it would be hard for him to raise the boys by himself, so before she died she made plans for her sons to be taken care of by a guardian, Mrs. Blass, who lived in Chula Vista.

Don remembered seeing his father only on the weekends during this time. That is when he would visit the boys and bring them presents; clothes or games. He always brought art supplies for Don. Sunday was Don's favorite day because that was when he was able to spend long hours with his dad. Sometime after this they all moved back to San Diego to a little house on Kalmia Street.

Now, on Saturday afternoons, Don was able to visit his father at the clothing store where his father worked. Don spent time there sketching the customers as they shopped. On Saturday nights he would have dinner with his father and then sometimes they would see a play together. His father loved the theatre and would take Don with him whenever there was a new show in town.

When Don was ten his father gave him a shiny brass trumpet for Christmas. This was just what Don wanted! He wasn't able to take lessons, though. Instead he learned by listening to records and trying to play along with the orchestra. *"Whenever Mrs. Blass went out of the house I turned on the records and sat next to the victrola and blew myself red in the face."*

When Don Freeman graduated from high school, he thought he would go to New York City to start living his own life. But his grandmother surprised him with a special graduation gift: art lessons for the whole summer at the San Diego School of Fine Arts.

All during this time he continued to play the trumpet. Even while he was studying what he really loved - art - he remembered that **"once in a while I found myself torn between a life of playing the horn and a life using a pencil."**

In 1929 Don finally left for New York. As he traveled across the United States he earned money by playing his trumpet. When he finally arrived in the "Big Apple" his first job was playing his horn at a wedding reception for eleven dollars.

For the next year he supported himself by playing the trumpet but he also continued studying at the Art Student's League. He loved sketching what he found around New York; streets, stores, tall buildings, and people. People, people, people, people. He sketched them **"carrying signs, fishing for change through sidewalk gratings, shining shoes, peddling gardenias, selling corsets, plugging hit songs, washing windows, sharpening knives."** This was the perfect place for an artist! He filled many sketch pads with sights of the city.

All this time he still tried to decide whether he should be a musician or an artist. He never really did decide by himself what to do. Once he was riding the subway, he got so involved in sketching that he almost missed his stop. He rushed off the train clutching his sketch pad. As the train pulled away he suddenly realized his horn was still on the train! That was that. Now he had to be an artist.

He began drawing pictures of actors and scenery at Broadway shows. He sold these drawings to newspapers and they were published. He loved this kind of work. He was paid for going to see the shows and he was paid for the pictures he drew of them.

In 1931 Don Freeman married Lydia Cooley, an artist he met during those summer art lessons in San Diego. They liked living in New York very much and they enjoyed going out sketching the city sights together. In 1943 Don began illustrating books for other writers. In the late 1940's he and his wife moved back to California where their son Roy was born.

In 1951 Don and Lydia published their first children's book, *Chuggy and the Blue Caboose*. Together they also created *Pet of the Met* which shows their drawings of the backstage at the Metropolitan Opera House. From then on, up until the time of his death on February 1, 1978, Don Freeman produced an average of one children's book a year.

Many people's favorite Don Freeman book is *Corduroy,* the story of the department store stuffed bear who finally finds a real home. *Beady Bear* and *Bearymore* are other popular Freeman books. If you enjoy animal stories you will want to read *Flash the Dash; Ski Pup; Come Again, Pelican; Dandelion* and many more.

Don Freeman probably would have made a fine jazz musician. But millions of readers are secretly happy that he lost his trumpet on the train that day. He must have been too, because he once said, ***"Creating picture books for children fulfills all my enthusiasms and interests and love of life."*** And are we glad!

A Selection of Books by Don Freeman

It Shouldn't Happen	A Rainbow of My Own
Come One, Come All!	The Guard Mouse
Chuggy and the Blue Caboose	Add-A-Line Alphabet
Pet of the Met	Corduroy
Beady Bear	Tilly Witch
Mop Top	Quiet! There's a Canary in the Library
Fly High, Fly Low	Forever Laughter
The Night The Lights Went Out	Hattie the Backstage Bat
Norman the Doorman	Penguins of All People!
Space Witch	Inspector Peckit
Cyrano the Crow	Flash the Dash
Come Again, Pelican	The Paper Party
Ski Pup	The Seal and the Slick
Botts, the Naughty Otter	Will's Quill
The Turtle and the Dove	The Chalk Box Story
Dandelion	A Pocket for Corduroy

PATRICIA REILLY GIFF

Patricia Reilly Giff says that she was bitten by the reading bug when she was ***"probably around four years old."*** She fondly remembers sitting in a big soft chair with her mother or father as they read to her on long winter nights. Her favorite book was *Little Women,* but she also loved *Hiawatha, Evangeline, Secret Garden,* and *Jane Eyre.* While her friends played hide and seek, Patricia sat under a cherry tree reading.

She grew up in St. Albins, a suburb of New York City. The librarian there was very helpful, Patricia says, ***"choosing wonderful things for me to read. I read the stories of my mother's childhood and every book in our little library in St. Albin's."*** Today the librarian is in her nineties and Patricia still keeps in touch with her. What a thrill it must be for both of them to continue to share books. . .especially Patricia Reilly Giff's books!

When Patricia was growing up and going to school, she prepared herself to become a school teacher. She taught in various public schools from 1956 to 1984. By this time she was married to James A. Giff and had three children: James, William, and Alice. All this time, though, what she really wanted most was to be a writer. ***"I always wanted to be a writer. Always."***

You can only become a writer by writing. Patricia Reilly Giff had finished college, she had taught school, she had married and raised a family, she had turned 40 years old and realized that she hadn't even tried to write a story. To be a writer, you must write. So Patricia decided to start writing. She thought about the children she had worked with in school and wrote for them.

In 1979 she had two books published. In 1980 she had three more published and there has been a steady stream of delightful stories ever since. One of her latest is *Mother Teresa: Sister to the Poor.*

When asked which of her books is her favorite, she does not hesitate one bit: *The Gift of the Pirate Queen.* ***"It was written for my son who has diabetes."*** It's the story of Grace O'Malley and her little sister, Amy. The two girls are still adjusting to the death of their mother and, to make matters worse, their father has invited a cousin from Ireland to stay with them for a while till things get back to normal. Well, cousin Fiona is a spinner of tales and. . . you will have to read the book to find out all about the Pirate Queen, her ship the *"White Horse"*, and her gift to Grace. Also notice the dedication in the front of the book: *"for James Matthew Giff with love."*

Some of Mrs. Giff's most popular books are about the Adventures of Casey Valentine and her friends: *Fourth-Grade Celebrity, The Girl Who Knew It All, Left-Handed Shortstop,* and *The Winter Worm Business.* For younger readers there are *"The Kids of Polk Street School"* books. In the one called *Say "Cheese"* Emily Arrow learns that instead of having just one best friend, *"It's better to have a couple of different ones."* If you enjoy playing with your friends and going to school together, you will love the *"Kids of the Polk Street School."*

When she started writing, Mrs. Giff would get up very early on dark cold mornings, fix herself a big pot of tea, and work away while everyone else was still sleeping. *"It was hard. It was really so hard. But then I began to feel the joy of it, learning as I wrote, laughing. . . ."* She writes at home every day now and her husband is the first one to read her books.

Besides writing, she enjoys needlepoint, geneaology, and reading. Her favorite foods are potatoes and *"chocolate anything!"*

Patricia Reilly Giff often visits schools to share her stories with the students. When asked what she likes best about these visits, she answers with enthusiasm: *"The Kids!"*

A Selection of Books by Patricia Reilly Giff

Almost Awful Play	Love, From The Fifth Grade Celebrity
Beast In Ms. Rooney's Room	Mother Teresa: Sister To The Poor
Candy Corn Contest	Mystery Of The Blue Ring
Columbus Circle	Pickle Puss
December Secrets	Poopsie Pomerantz, Pick Up Your Feet
Fish Face	Powder Puff Puzzle
Fourth Grade Celebrity	Purple Climbing Days
Gift Of The Pirate Queen	Rat Teeth
Girl Who Knew It All	Red Purse Riddle
Happy Birthday, Ronald Morgan	Say "Cheese"
Have You Seen Hyacinth Macaw?	Secrets At The Polk Street School
In The Dinosaur's Paw	Snaggle Doodles
Laura Ingalls Wilder: Growing Up In The Little House	Sunny Side Up
Lazy Lions, Lucky Lambs	Today Was A Terrible Day
Left Handed Shortstop	Valentine Star
Loretta P. Sweeny, Where Are You?	Watch Out, Ronald Morgan!
	Winter Worm Business

PAUL GOBLE

Paul Goble's books and paintings are about Native American Indian people who lived on the Great Plains region of the United States. He has loved reading about the Native American Indians since he was a young boy. He has deliberately chosen to write and illustrate books for children rather than adults because he wants to share his understanding and knowledge with readers who might not know much about Native American ways or who might have confused ideas about them from watching television or movies. He also hopes that his books will be further encouragement for Indian children to be proud of their own tribal traditions.

Children of all colors and backgrounds seem to love his stories. *The Girl Who Loved Wild Horses,* which won the Caldecott Medal in 1979 for being the best American picture book, and other works of his have been translated into several different languages so children in non-English speaking countries can also enjoy learning about Native Americans.

In his books, Paul Goble often depicts humans and animals as living in two worlds which are connected. His own life has been somewhat like this. From his books you might think that he is a Native American, but he was born and raised in England. He lived with his parents and brother in an area where there were woods, gardens, and ponds. He loved nature and the outdoors and would spend hours playing imaginative games. Looking for buried treasure, climbing a high tree to light a warning lantern in the mast of his pretend *"tree ship"* every evening, camping under the tree in a waterproof *"house"*, dressing up in pirate and Indian clothes, and listening to stories read by his mother almost every night were some of the things he did as a boy in England. His favorite books then were *Treasure Island (pirates)* and stories by Grey Owl and Ernest Thompson Seton *(wildlife and Indians).*

His parents love classical music and everyone in the family plays an instrument. His father makes harpsichords. His mother is a musician and painter. As a family they played recorders together for many years.

As a child Paul Goble loved to watch, identify and draw birds. He was a member of three bird watching societies and spent hours and hours identifying new birds. He was even given special permission to enter a twenty-acre migratory area where some rarely seen birds lived. The officials who gave him permission to be there knew that he could be trusted not to damage any nests or harm the birds in any way. Besides watching live birds, Paul loved to draw stuffed birds which he saw in the glass cases inside a museum near his home. The museum curator would bring the stuffed bird that Paul wished to draw that day to a table and he would try to draw it. *"Drawing is the hardest thing I know,"* he says. *"Nobody can teach anyone to draw; you have to just work at it. I went to art college but I did not learn to draw there. It just means trying again and again."*

Besides drawing birds, every year at Christmas time Paul would paint 25-30 Christmas cards for his family to send to relatives and friends. He was also a collector of pressed flowers, stamps, rocks, and stone age artifacts. His parents gave him part of the garage which became a 'museum' for his many collections. Today he still takes great joy in collecting and identifying stamps, birds, and pressed flowers in his adopted country, the United States. He loves nature and works at home in a studio that has windows on three sides giving him a view of the forest and wildlife outside.

Before Paul Goble became an author illustrator he was an industrial designer and teacher in England. One day his son, Richard, was watching a program on British television about General Custer that had no basis in fact. Paul went to the library to find a children's book about Custer and the Indians that would be an accurate account and finding none he decided to write one himself. *Red Hawk's Account of Custer's Last Stand* was the result.

In 1972 he began a series of summertime camping trips with Richard to the United States to visit the Sioux, Crow, and Shoshoni reservations in South Dakota and Montana. On these trips he participated in many of their tribal activities, listening and learning about the old ways. His books are records of a great people and are gifts to them as well as to all of us. In 1977 Paul made a permanent move to South Dakota where he now lives with his wife, Janet, and younger son, Robert. Several of his books are dedicated to them. Robert is eight and is an enthusiastic encourager of his father's work. Richard is a grown-up and is a doctor in London. Paul Goble also has a grown-up daughter, Julia, who works in London.

Today Paul, Janet, and Robert Goble live in the Black Hills of South Dakota where they are close to nature, wildlife, and Native American lands and people. Their pets are the creatures of the forest. Robert goes to school and Paul and Janet work at home. Paul Goble is happy to be living here and is now a United States citizen. He is also an adopted member of the Sioux and Yakima tribes. He writes, *"I feel that I have seen and learned many wonderful things from Indian people, which most people would never have the opportunity to experience. I have simply wanted to express and to share these things which I love so much."*

You have, you have, Paul Goble. Thank you so much!

Selected Books By Paul Goble

Red Hawk's Account of Custer's Last Stand
Brave Eagle's Account of The Fetterman Fight
The Friendly Wolf
Lone Bull's Horse Raid
The Girl Who Loved Wild Horses
The Gift of the Sacred Dog
Star Boy
Buffalo Women
The Great Race of the Birds and Animals
Death of the Iron Horse
Her Seven Brothers
Iktomi and the Boulder
Iktomi and the Berries
Beyond the Ridge
Dream Wolf

THE GIRL WHO LOVED WILD HORSES

SYD HOFF

Syd Hoff grew up in New York City, the son of Benjamin and Mary Hoff. While he was going to school he was always interested in art. When he graduated from high school he studied at the National Academy of Design. His instructors there noticed a **"comical"** touch to his artwork and encouraged him to do something else with his talent. So he turned to doing cartoons. At the age of 18 he sold his first cartoon to *The New Yorker* magazine. That was over 50 years ago and since then he has contributed many cartoons to many different magazines.

From 1939 to 1949 Syd Hoff drew a daily comic strip about a little girl named Tuffy which ran in lots of newspapers. She was always doing funny things that made people laugh.

Nearly every child has read and enjoyed *Danny and the Dinosaur.* This was Mr. Hoff's very first *I CAN READ* book. It was published in 1958. In 1969 it was translated into Spanish as *Danielito y el Dinosauro.* The book has also been made into a popular filmstrip.

Thunderhoof, which is dedicated to Mr. Hoff's father, is the story of a wild horse who runs happy and free. Then he is captured by cowboys who take him back to the ranch. The cowboys try, but they can't tame Thunderhoof. So they let him go again. But now the horse is not as happy as before. It misses the cowboys. Luckily, the story does not end there. If you love horses you will love *Thunderhoof.*

Henrietta Goes to the Fair, dedicated to **"Dutch, my blue ribbon wife,"** tells about Farmer Gray's friendly barnyard animals who would just love to win the prize ribbon at the fair. Everyone thinks that Winthrop, Mr. Gray's biggest pig, is sure to win, but things just don't seem to work out that way. Sometimes prizes are won by the one least expecting to win!

Mr. Hoff is a concerned citizen interested in a clean and healthy environment. *The Litter Knight,* published in 1970, tells how Sir Dudley and his friends the Dragons teach the king and everyone in the land the importance of taking good care of the land. That is still a valuable lesson for all of us.

Syd Hoff has written and illustrated more than 20 books in his long career. He also illustrates books by other writers.

Don't Be My Valentine, written by Joan Lexau, is a funny story about Sam, Amy Lou, their teacher Mrs. Plum, and the other boys and girls in their class. You have probably enjoyed making and giving Valentines to your friends. Well, how would you feel if you opened one that said:

"*Roses are red*

Violets are blue

How did you ever

Get out of the zoo?"

Read this book with its Syd Hoff illustrations to find out who sent this Valentine and why.

Albert Albatross, Walpole, Chester, Grizzwold, Julius, Little Chief, Sammy Seal, Stanley. . . . the list of Syd Hoff characters goes on and on. Reading his books is like eating peanuts. Once you've read one, you won't want to stop until you've read them all!

A Selection of Books by Syd Hoff

Albert the Albatross
Barkley
The Horse in Harry's Room
Santa's Moose
Thunderhoof
Walpole
Who Will Be My Friends?
Chester
Danny and the Dinosaur
Grizzwold
Julius
Little Chief
Oliver
Sammy the Seal
Stanley
Barney's Horse
Mrs. Brice's Mice
Syd Hoff Animal Jokes
When Will It Snow?
Lengthy
How to Draw Cartoons

CAROLYN KEENE

Carolyn Keene, author of the *Nancy Drew* mystery books is something of a mystery herself. You won't find information about her on book jackets or in any author reference books found in most libraries. However, the mystery of this author can begin to be solved by learning that her real name was Harriet S. Adams. She only used Carolyn Keene as her pseudonym or pen name to write the *Nancy Drew* and *Dana Girls* stories. She was born in Newark, New Jersey and lived in Maplewood, N.J. for most of her life.

Her father, Edward Stratemeyer founded the Stratemeyer Syndicate which was a company that hired writers to create hundreds of different books for boys and girls from ideas that he and other people had. Books such as the *Hardy Boys, the Dana Girls,* and the *Nancy Drews* were all published by his company. The first three *Nancy Drew* mystery books were Mr. Stratemeyer's idea and were published before he died in 1930. They became immediately popular with young readers, outselling every other girl detective series book around.

Harriet Adams *(Carolyn Keene)* had wanted to be an author since she was a little girl and when she graduated from college she went to work for her father's book writing syndicate. After he died the *Nancy Drew* books became her project and remained so for fifty years. She also found time to supervise the writing and publishing of another mystery series called *The Dana Girls* where she used her Carolyn Keene pseudonym as the author's name again. The *Dana Girls* series lasted for thirty-five years but never became as popular as the *Nancy Drew* books.

Books with different titles that use the same main characters over and over again are called series books. In the *Nancy Drew* series, the main or ***"stock"*** characters are Nancy, who lives with her *"famous lawyer"* father, Carson Drew, and an *"elderly housekeeper"*, Hannah Gruen. Nancy's mother is dead. Her friends Bess, George, and Ned share in many adventures but it is Nancy who is able to solve the mysteries by smart detective work. This is the plot formula that has worked so well for almost sixty years. Three generations of girls have loved reading the Nancy Drew books and seventy million copies in fourteen languages have been sold!

Besides being a writer, Harriet Adams taught Sunday school and enjoyed working as a volunteer with the Red Cross and the Girl Scouts. Imagine how fun it would have been to have her as a Girl Scout leader! She liked to play the piano and collect dolls and was also interested in farming and gardening. She raised beautiful plants and flowers in her greenhouse. Nancy Drew travels to many different countries and so did Harriet Adams. She loved to travel and made many trips throughout the world to research story settings for a new book. She was married and had three children and eventually ten grandchildren and three great grandchildren. Harriet Adams died on March 27, 1982.

Readers may be curious to know why some of the Nancy Drews have different covers and are now appearing in a paperback series called, *"The Nancy Drew Files."* In 1984 after Harriet Adams died, her books and the Carolyn Keene pen name were sold to a different publishing company who wanted to update some of the old stories in order to make them more interesting and believable to today's young readers. The plots in the *"Nancy Drew Files"* mysteries are more complicated and frightening. Currently these new paperbacks are being published at a rate of one a month.

Readers may have seen another new mystery series in paperback featuring Nancy Drew and the Hardy Boys working together. So, even though Harriet Adams has died other writers have permission to use **her** characters and **their** imaginations to keep the Nancy Drew detective series going.

Why have these books been popular for so long? That really isn't a difficult mystery to solve. First of all, they are easy to read and understand. Nancy explains everything! She is also a very likeable character; friendly, modest, and independent. She solves most problems by herself without a great deal of assistance from adults. The best clue to the Nancy Drew success story is that each chapter ends in such an exciting way that the readers can't wait to find out what will happen next!

Before she died Harriet Adams organized a *Nancy Drew Cookbook* which featured recipes that use familiar names, places or even book titles from her mystery series.There are recipes for *"Crumbling Wall Coffee Cake," "Blackwood Hall Muffins," "Bungalow Mystery Salad," "Shadow Ranch Barbecued Beans"* and a hundred more. The book offers ideas for holiday cooking, picnics, breakfasts, and adding mysterious flavors to recipes. This is a fun book to check out of the library!

Has the Carolyn Keene mystery been solved for those of you who wanted information about this famous author? We know for certain that someone named Harriet Adams really lived and worked in New Jersey for many years using Carolyn Keene as a pen name to write many of the *Nancy Drew* books. Just which ones she wrote by herself we don't know for sure because many other people worked on the books with her. Her father did the first three Nancy Drews and she played an important part in creating the next sixty-six before she retired. She didn't leave her fans with many clues about her life but she did leave us an exciting mystery series to read. Best of all, Nancy Drew, girl detective, continues to have new adventures to solve in the world of books.

Nancy Drew Mystery Stories by Carolyn Keene

The Secret of the Old Clock
The Hidden Staircase
The Bungalow Mystery
Mystery at Lilac Inn
The Secret of Shadow Ranch
The Secret of Red Gate Farm
The Clue in the Diary
Nancy's Mysterious Letter
The Sign of the Twisted Candles
Password to Larkspur Lane
The Clue to the Broken Locket
The Message in the Hollow Oak
Mystery of the Ivory Charm
The Whispering Statue
The Haunted Bridge
The Clue of the Tapping Heels
Mystery of the Brass-Bound Trunk
Mystery of the Moss Covered Mansion
The Quest of the Missing Cap
The Clue in the Jewel Box
The Secret in the Old Attic
The Clue in the Crumbling Wall
Mystery of the Tolling Bell
The Clue in the Old Album
The Ghost of Blackwell Hall
The Clue of the Leaning Chimney
The Secret of the Wooden Lady
The Clue of the Black Keys
Mystery at the Ski Jump
The Clue of the Velvet Mask
The Ringmaster's Secret
The Scarlet Slippery Mystery
The Witch Tree Mystery
The Haunted Showboat

The Secret of the Golden Pavilion
The Clue in the Old Stagecoach
The Mystery of the Fire Dragon
The Clue of the Dancing Puppet
The Moonstone Castle Mystery
The Clue of the Whistling Bagpipes
The Phantom of Pine Hill
The Mystery of the 99 Steps
The Clue in the Crossword Cipher
The Spider Sapphire Mystery
The Invisible Intruder
The Mysterious Mannequin
The Crooked Banister
The Secret of Mirror Bay
The Double Jinx Mystery
Mystery of the Glowing Eye
The Secret of the Forgotten City
The Sky Phantom
The Strange Message in the Parchment
Mystery of Crocodile Island
The Thirteenth Pearl
The Triple Hoax
The Flying Saucer Mystery
The Secret in the Old Lace
The Greek Symbol Mystery
The Swami's Ring
The Kachina Doll Mystery
The Twin Dilemma
Captive Witness
Mystery of the Winged Lion
Race Against Time
The Sinister Omen
The Elusive Heiress
Clue in the Ancient Disguise

The Jokers Revenge
Secret of Shady Glen
Mystery of Misty Canyon
Case of the Rising Stars
Search for Cindy Austin
The Bluebeard Room
Case of the Disappearing Diamonds
Case of the Vanishing Veil

Clue in the Camera
Double Horror of Fenley Place
The Enemy Match
The Eskimo's Secret
The Haunted Carousel
The Mardi Gras Mystery
The Phantom of Venice
The Emerald Eyed Cat

ASTRID LINDGREN

The famous author of the *Pippi Longstocking* books lives in Sweden. She was born there in 1907 to parents who were farmers. She says that she cannot imagine anybody having a happier childhood than she did with lots of books, interesting people, animals, and a woods to play in whenever she wished. In those days there were no automobiles, movies, or television but children like Astrid Lindgren used their imaginations to invent wonderful ways to amuse themselves. These memories of her childhood often appear later in her stories. She doesn't live on a farm any longer but often returns there for visits to get story ideas.

When Asrid Lindgren finished high school she went to Stockholm, the capital city of Sweden, to learn to be a secretary. Later she worked in a newspaper office, married and had two children. She did not plan to become a writer although people were always telling her that she would be an author someday. She liked to make up stories to tell her young children and their friends. Her daughter's favorite story character was someone they called *"Pippi Langstrump"* now known as *"Pippi Longstocking."*

One winter day as Astrid Lindgren was walking on a Stockholm street, she slipped on ice and broke her ankle. The doctor made her stay in bed and she was bored! To keep busy she began to write down the *Pippi* stories and that was the beginning of her writing career.

Pippi Longstocking was written in Swedish but has been translated into twenty-four other languages. No one knows how many millions of copies of the Pippi books have been sold throughout the world. Several million have been sold in the United States alone. Four full-length color films and many videos about Pippi have also been made. If you visit Sweden you will see posters advertising them. Pippi Longstocking is a movie star there! In Swedish bookstores and libraries there are shelves of Astrid Lindgren's books on display. She is one of Sweden's most popular writers.

This author has written more than 115 books for young readers and has received many important awards for them. Some of her books are written for children as young as three years old but most of them are for readers who are ages eight to twelve.

Besides the Pippi books she has written a detective series *(Bill Bergson)*, a series about a mischievous boy named Emil who gets into trouble no matter what he does, and stories about children who live in places called Noisy Village and Troublemaker Street.

Her book characters often live without parents or other adults. They seem to be able to do almost anything they want and they get into lots of trouble as a result. ***"Pippi is a nine year old orphan with hair the color of a carrot, a nose shaped like a very small potato, and lots of freckles. She can stuff herself with fourteen cookies anytime she wants."*** 'Ronia' the robber's daughter, lives with a band of robbers deep in the woods where she climbs steep cliffs, jumps over waterfalls, and runs away from angry gray dwarfs. Most of Astrid Lindgren's story characters have one thing in common. They are fearless!

Astrid Lindgren's books are always written first in Swedish and then translated into other languages. She uses a time-saving method of writing called shorthand which she learned in secretarial school. She rewrites each chapter many times before typing the final version. Her books are illustrated with drawings or paintings but she does not illustrate them herself.

Today her two children are grown up and she has seven grandchildren. She lives in Stockholm and also has a vacation house on the Baltic Sea, not far from the city. She cares a great deal about children, nature, and animals. Recently, she has been helping people in the Swedish government to pass laws which will protect and improve the care of farm animals. These new laws will prevent cattle, pigs, and chickens from being caged, tethered, or treated with hormones to make them grow faster.

Even though she is eighty-two years old and has been a famous author for many years, Astrid Lindgren has no intention of retiring. She continues to write books for children and works on television and movie films too. Her fans all over the world are glad to hear that she will be telling us more stories!

A Selection of Books Written by Astrid Lindgren

Pippi Longstocking
Pippi Goes on Board
Pippi in the South Seas
Bill Bergson, Master Detective
Bill Bergson Lives Dangerously
Bill Bergson and the White Rose Rescue
Mio, My Son
Rasmus and the Vagabond
Mischievous Meg
The Children of Noisy Village
Happy Times in Noisy Village
Christmas in Noisy Village
Springtime in Noisy Village
Pippi on the Run
The Brothers Lionheart
Christmas in the Stable
Emil and Piggy Beast
Emil in Soup Tureen
Emil's Pranks
I want a Brother or Sister
Karlsson-on-the-Roof
Lotta on Troublemaker Street
Mischievous Meg
Of Course Polly Can Ride A Bike
Seacrow Island
The Children of Troublemaker Street
The Tomten
The Tomten and The Fox
I Don't Want To Go To Bed
I Want To Go To School Too

LEO LIONNI

Leo Lionni is as famous for his advertising and design work as he is for his books for children. His first children's book, **Little Blue and Little Yellow,** was written in 1959 for his grandchildren during a dull train ride. It is about two scraps of colored paper; one blue, one yellow, who play together across the pages and eventually come together in a hug to create a new color. Of all the books that he has done, he says that he is the proudest of the first page of this book.

Leo Lionni can paint, draw, sculpt, create mosaics, design, play the guitar, and write! He was born in Holland in 1910. He did not have formal art lessons but he spent much of his free time as a child in two fine art museums near his home teaching himself to draw. When he was growing up there was no television. His school emphasized nature studies which became a lifelong interest for him. He kept a collection of small animals, mostly reptiles, in terrariums at home. Today he loves to write books about animals; mice, lizards, rabbits, snakes, snails, chameleons, and crocodiles.

The animals in Lionni's books do not look like photographs of real animals. They are colorful and simply drawn. Many look alike, having the same ears, bodies, and legs. Their eyes and mouths are what give them individuality. Mice are some of his favorite characters and he has written several books about them. *Alexander and the Wind-Up Mouse, Geraldine the Music Mouse, Frederick,* and *The Green Tail Mouse* are four Lionni stories featuring mice.

Leo Lionni's animals have the same feelings that people have. His stories are about friendship, choices, acceptance, and being yourself. He likes to write animal fables that help us to understand ourselves and our world a little better. Four of his picture books have won Caldecott Honor awards. They all have silver medals on their covers if you go looking for them in your library. Several of his books have received other important book awards and some have been made into animated films for television.

The question that people most frequently ask him is, *"How do you get your ideas, Mr. Lionni?" "He answers that most people seem to think that getting an idea is both mysterious and simple yet it isn't at all. Creating a book takes place slowly, by trial and error and is hard, disciplined work."*

Leo Lionni lived in several European countries before moving to America in 1939. Here he worked as a designer and art director in Philadelphia and New York. He became a naturalized citizen in 1945. In 1947 he began to seriously work at painting. His oils and watercolors have been exhibited in many art galleries in Europe, Asia, and the United States. Now he concentrates mainly on creating picture books and on projects connected with them such as television films.

Leo Lionni and his wife, Nora, have two grown-up sons, two grandchildren and two homes. One home is in New York City and the other is in Sienna, Italy. He likes living in such different places. His New York home is an apartment in the middle of the city and his Italian home overlooks the sea where animals and woods are nearby.

In 1985 when he was seventy-five years old his publisher gave him a very special birthday present. Thirteen of his best-loved animal fables were collected into one beautiful volume and published again with a new title, *FREDERICK'S FABLES: A Leo Lionni Treasury.* Like his famous character, Frederick, Leo Lionni had been gathering words and *"when he finished, they all applauded as he shyly took a bow."*

Selected Books By Leo Lionni

Little Blue, and Little Yellow	Geraldine, The Music Mouse
Inch by Inch	Let's Make Rabbits
Swimmy	Cornelius
Tico and the Golden Wings	When?
Frederick	Where?
Alexander and the Wind-Up Mouse	What?
The Biggest House in the World	Who?
The Alphabet Tree	Words to Talk About
Fish is Fish	Numbers to Talk About
Theodore and the Talking Mushroom	Letters to Talk About
In the Rabbit Garden	Colors to Talk About
Pezzettino	Frederick's Fables: A Leo Lionni Treasury
A Color of His Own	It's Mine!
I want to Stay Here! I want to Go There! A Flea Story	Tillie and the Wall

LOIS LOWRY

Lois Lowry is a loving woman and writer. She does not write picture books, so you may have to wait a while to get to know the characters who live in her stories. But you will definitely read them as soon as you are able. Lois Hammersberg was born in Honolulu before Hawaii became a state. Her father was a dentist and her mother had been a teacher before she had a family. Lois had one sister who died when she was in her twenties.

While she was going to college, she met and fell in love with Donald Grey Lowry. She left college before she finished to marry Donald. She was nineteen. By the time she was twenty-five she had four children: Alix, Greg, Kristin, and Benjamin. As a young mother she found she had lots of energy. She could **"change a diaper with one hand, write a magazine article with the other and stir spaghetti sauce in between."** When her children were older, she returned to college to graduate.

Lois' interest in writing started at a very early age. She had taught herself to read when she was three and she still remembers the feeling of excitement she had when she first realized that letters made sounds and that sounds made words and that words made sentences and that sentences made stories. **"I was very young. . . not yet four years old. It was then that I decided that one day I would write books."**

Since her father was away at the War when she was little, she only remembers her mother reading to her sister and her. Her favorite books were *Mary Poppins* and *(later) The Yearling*.

During the War her family moved to a small residential neighborhood in Carlisle, Pennsylvania. She recalls that there were **"bumpy sidewalks where we played hopscotch and jumped rope and rollerskated. The houses had front porches and the people sat on them on summer evenings while the children ran across the lawns, catching lightning bugs."**

She has an excellent memory, as you can tell. Her memory is partly what makes her such a good writer. She can just **"push a button"** in her mind and she can be five years old, or eight, or ten, or whatever age she is writing about. Her books are not about her, though many of her stories have things happen in them that are like things that have really happened to her. Her memories of how she felt at certain times help her write about them as though they happen for real. One example of this is Lois' book *A Summer to Die* which is based on her memories of when her sister died of cancer.

Some of her funniest stories are about a little girl named Anastasia Krupnik. ***"She's probably a mixture of my two quite nutty daughters,"*** says Lois. Readers who love Anastasia and her family have watched her grow from ten years old to thirteen years old.

The first book, *Anastasia Krupnik,* introduces the freckle-faced girl whose father, Myron, is a college professor and poet and whose mother, Katherine, is an artist. Her little brother Sam is a genius. Anastasia and her family are always getting into funny situations. In *Anastasia, Ask Your Analyst,* she is turning into a teenager. . . YUCK! But her family loves her through the pains of growing up. The latest book, *Anastasia's Chosen Career,* tells of thirteen year old Anastasia, a troublesome school project and a new friend she makes during winter vacation. As long as Lois Lowry keeps writing about Anastasia, boys and girls will keep reading about her.

Lois Lowry and her husband were divorced in 1977 . She now works out of her apartment in the Beacon Hill area of Boston. She writes at her desk for about five hours every day. Part of the time she spends writing to students who are learning how to become writers, part of the time is spent answering fan mail from children and grownups, and the rest of the time is spent writing stories. And are we glad!

When she is not writing she likes to ***"knit, grow flowers, cook, read, listen to music, travel, take pictures, and go to movies."*** Her favorite food is ***"Mexican food. . . any kind."*** Her favorite place is the 150 year old farmhouse in rural New Hampshire where she spends most weekends. She is not very athletic, but she loves to watch professional football on television.

When asked to share her favorite memory, Lois Lowry admits that she has many, and that probably most of them have to do with her children when they were very young. . . they are all in their twenties now.

"One memory that comes to my mind is a day long ago when I was in a small grocery store with my daughter Alix, then four years old. A drunk entered the

39

store, lurching and stumbling. . . . all of us who were there moved away as he passed, and looked at him with disgust. All but my daughter. She watched him curiously for a moment. . . . then she walked over, took his hand, and said, 'Here. I'll help you.' It is hard to forget that kind of genuine sweetness which most of us outgrow too soon."

Lois Lowry has not outgrown that sweetness and we are sure she never will.

Selected Books By Lois Lowry

A Summer to Die
Find a Stranger, Say Goodbye
Anatasia Krupnik
Autumn Street
Anastasia Again!
Anastasia at Your Service
Taking Care of Terrific
Anastasia, Ask Your Analyst
Us and Uncle Fraud
Anastasia's Chosen Career
Rabble Starkey
Anastasia Has the Answer
Anastasia On Her Own
One Hundredth Thing About Caroline
Switcharound
All About Sam
Number the Stars

Things I Love !	Things I Hate !
Making Lists	Mr. Belden (at the drugstore)
Mounds Bars	~~Boys~~
Writing Poems	Liver
My Room	Pumpkin Pie
My Wart	Mrs. Westvessel
Frank (my goldfish)	~~My Parents~~
Secret Bad Thoughts	Babies
Wedding Gowns	Boys
~~Washburn Cummings~~	Washburn Cummings
My Name	~~All My Friends~~
My Grandmother	~~My Name~~
My Friends	
Wordsworth	
Christmas	

ROBERT McCLOSKEY

"Make way for Robert McCloskey!"

Robert McCloskey was born and grew up in Hamilton, Ohio. He remembers that from the time his fingers were long enough to play a scale, he took piano lessons. He also learned to play the harmonica, the drums, and the oboe. He thought he would like to be a musician when he grew up.

But then he became interested in mechanical things: electric motors, pieces of wire, and old clock springs. He built model trains and cranes with remote controls. Even the family Christmas tree had gadgets on it to make it turn and twirl and flash and buzz. He thought he might like to be an inventer.

But besides being musical and being mechanical, Robert McCloskey was very artistic. When he was a boy there were always lots of brushes, paints, and crayons lying around the house. So, naturally, he tried his hand at these. By the time he was in high school he was so good that his drawings appeared in the school annual.

When he graduated from high school he won a scholarship to the Vesper George Art School in Boston. It was while he was living in Boston around the corner from the Public Gardens that he first noticed a family of ducks living there. He watched them paddling around in the lake, waddling along the sidewalk, and even causing quite a traffic jam as they crossed the busy street. But that's a story that had to wait a while to be told.

When Robert was nineteen years old, his old hometown of Hamilton asked him to make some decorations for the outside of their municipal building. As a young boy he had enjoyed carving soap and wood, but this job was carving stone. He finished the project in just six months.

He traveled to New York where he became a student at the National Academy of Design. His art work there won many awards. Then for two summers he painted on Cape Cod in Massachusetts. He did not sell any oil paintings, but he did sell a few water colors. Soon he turned his talents to children's books.

The art he was doing was good, but it was not yet quite right for children's books. An editor suggested that he work with what he knew best, so he eventually moved back to Ohio. This was exactly the change that he needed for his art. He worked on a story and pictures about a little boy and his harmonica in a little midwestern town. He sold the book to a publisher during his very next visit to New York.

Next he went to work painting with a famous artist in Boston. It was during this stay in Boston that he got the idea for *Make Way For Ducklings.* This time he had the feeling that the ducks were just *"waiting around to be put into a picture book."* So he started doing just that.

He bought four mallard ducks and brought them to his apartment. He wanted to be able to draw them so that they really looked real. He followed them around with his sketchpad watching every move they made. He says that he had to learn to even *"think like a duck"* to be able to do the book right. He made many sketches of the ducks and the Boston sights which appear in the book. In 1942, after four years of thinking about the book and two more years of actually working on it, it was published and awarded the Caldecott Medal for the best picture book published in that year. Today, children who visit the park can climb on bronze statues of the mallard ducks which were placed there in 1987 to celebrate the book.

Writing and drawing what he knew best has really worked for Robert McClouskey. Two of his books, *Centerburg Tales* and *Homer Price ,* are filled with pictures inspired by hometown scenes, but also touched by McCloskey's talent and imagination. What he *"sees and draws"* sometimes surprises the neighbors who don't see the same thing in quite the same way.

In 1940 Robert McCloskey married Peggy Durand who is the daughter of a famous children's author. They had two daughters, Sally and Jane, who are both grown now. When they were little girls, even they found their way into their father's books. You will find them in *Blueberries for Sal* and *One Morning in Maine .*

The family lived for part of the year on an island in Maine where they had to go grocery shopping by boat. The generator and water pump always seemed to need repair and the barn became Mr. McCloskey's studio. It's no wonder that boats, water, weather, and nature scenes were always favorite subjects for his artwork. His first full-color picture book, *Time of Wonder* published in 1958, won him his second Caldecott Medal. Winning the Caldecott is a very great honor. Winning it twice is a very rare honor, indeed. But, then again, Robert McCloskey is a very rare artist, indeed.

Selected Books By Robert McCloskey

Blueberries for Sal
Burt Dow: Deep-Water Man
Centerburg Tales
Homer Price
Lentil
Make way for Ducklings
One Morning in Maine
Time of Wonder

MARY NORTON

Mary Norton was born on December 10, 1903 in London, England. When she was two years old her family moved out into the country. Their home had lots of space, beautiful lawns and gardens, a greenhouse, and a nearby river. When she was eight she went off to private school.

Mary had four brothers and it is interesting how this helped her much later with her writing career.

When she was a little girl and wanted to play with her brothers, they would often say, *"Stay here till we come back."* Well, for the longest time they would just leave her on her own. It was while they were off playing that she would notice all the little plants and rocks and holes and stems and leaves around her. She would imagine little creatures struggling through this great imaginary *"forest."*

She also remembers playing with her little imaginary china dolls. *"They stood about four inches high and were on sale among the lollipops in every village shop."* It was very easy to dress them up as different characters just using paint or cloth or bits of fur. She created knights, ladies, fairies, and even witches.

On rainy days when she would stay inside, she would play with her dolls under the furniture, near the fireplace, and in secret passageways. For tiny creatures, these were real adventures. At the time, she did not realize that her childhood play was preparing her for her career as a writer.

Some years later Mary had a brief acting career with the Old Vic Shakespeare Theater. She gave up acting at the age of twenty-four when she married Robert Charles Norton who was in the shipping business. She and her husband had four children: Ann, Robert, Guy, and Caroline. For more than ten years the family lived in Portugal because that was where Mr. Norton's business was. They lived way out in the country, *"but it was a paradise for children."*

When World War Two broke out the family moved back to England. For two years Mary worked in the British War Office. Then she was transferred to New York. She and the children stayed in a rented house in Connecticut. Because her job did not pay much, she began writing stories. She had often told the children bedtime stories and these stories gave her ideas for her books.

In 1943 they all moved back to London and while the bombs were landing on the city, Mary was busy writing. What she wrote became her first book, *The Magic Bed-Knob; or How to Become a Witch in Ten Easy Lessons.*

In 1945 Mary had a very frightening experience. During one of the London bombings her eyes were injured and she lost her sight. Fortunately an operation brought it back again. ***"The operation was successful and I remember driving home through sunlit streets, looking at the world through pin-point holes in blacked-out spectacles. . . and an exquisite world it was."***

Just a few years later she published *Bonfires and Broomsticks.* Later, a book publisher decided to combine both stories about the Wilson children *(The Magic Bed Knob* and *Bonfires and Broomstick)* into one volume with a new title, *Bed-Knob and Broomstick.* You may find this one book in your library instead of the other two.

Her most famous stories , though, are those about the wee people called the Borrowers. These are tiny people who resemble the little creatures she imagined when she was left by her brothers to ***"wait here, we'll be back for you."***

The Borrowers first appeared in 1952. Since then there have been six more Borrowers books. They are full of exciting adventures.

Her stories have been so well liked that in 1971 *Bed-knobs and Broomsticks* was made into a Walt Disney movie. *The Borrowers* was made into a television special in 1973.

The next time that your parents say, ***"Not now, I'm busy."*** or the next time your brother or sister says, ***"Later!"***, see what fantastic adventures you can invent. . . just like Mary Norton. Perhaps someday you will use them in a Borrowers story of your very own.

A Selection of Books By Mary Norton

The Magic Bed-knob; or How to Become a Witch in Ten Easy Lessons
Bonfires and Broomsticks
The Borrowers
The Borrowers Afield
The Borrowers Afloat
The Borrowers Aloft
Poor Stainless: A New Story about the Borrowers
Are All the Giants Dead?
Adventures of the Borrowers
Bed-knob and Broomsticks
The Borrowers Avenged

Illustration from *The Borrowers Aloft* by Mary Norton, Copyright © 1961
by Harcourt Brace Jovanovich, Inc., reproduced by permission of the publisher.

KATHERINE PATERSON

Katherine Paterson moves a lot! She was born in China where her father was a missionary and since then has had more than thirty homes in three countries. At the present time she is living in Barre, Vermont. She is married and has four children. Her daughters are adopted; Lin is Chinese and Mary is a Native American Indian. Her two sons, John and David, arrived in the regular way. She also has been a foster mother and this experience helped her write *The Great Gilly Hopkins,* the story of a foster child's search for her real mother.

Katherine taught herself to read before she went to school. She thinks this happened because she loved the stories and poems that her mother read to her every day. Reading is something she still loves. She says that she is not a fast reader but would rather read than do most anything.

This author can speak Japanese since she lived and worked in Japan before she was married. There she was a teacher and assistant to eleven country ministers. She used to ride a motorcycle from church to church because she didn't have a car. At one time she planned to live in Japan forever, but these plans changed when she returned to New York City to go back to college. There she met her future husband, John, and they were married the next year.

However, Japan remained an important part of her life as an author. One of her novels about Japan, *The Master Puppeteer,* won the National Book Award in 1977 making her a famous children's author. This book tells the story of an apprentice puppeteer who works for a harsh master in a famous and ancient Japanese puppet theater. She has written two other novels about Japan, *The Sign of the Chrysanthemum* and *Of Nightingales That Weep.*

Katherine Paterson started to write seriously when her children were very young. She didn't have a study or special place for writing in those days. She didn't have much time for writing either because she was a busy mother, but she did have her husband's strong encouragement. She wrote stories for nine years before selling one. During those years she went over and over her work, practicing and revising it until she was sure that it was the best she could do. Katherine has always cared about

47

excellence and does not want to ever do mediocre work or work that is second best.

When her children were young, they had lots of pets in the house. There were dogs, cats, gerbils, and even boa constrictors. Today the children are grown and the Patersons have only one pet, a dog named Princess.

Her children and husband have always played an important part in her writing. They read her stories before they are sent to the publisher and offer criticism and advice, although she doesn't always listen to them. Sometimes when things happen to her children they find their way into her books. After her son David's best friend, Lisa, was accidentally killed by lightning she wrote *Bridge to Terabithia* to help him and the entire family recover from the tragedy. *Bridge to Terabithia* is not the story of David Paterson and his friend Lisa but it is the story of a wonderful friendship, a secret kingdom and a terrible accident. *Bridge to Terabithia* won the Newbery Medal in 1978 and continues to be widely read. Many readers consider it to be their favorite Katherine Paterson book. It has been adapted for television as has *The Great Gilly Hopkins* which was a Newbery Honor book in 1979, the year after *Bridge* won the Newbery Medal.

This famous author's books take one to three years to research and write and then another year to get published. Ideas for them come from many different places. She says that she can't choose a favorite from those she has already written because they are like her children; she loves them all.

It is unusual for one author to write so many award winning books in a row in such a relatively few years. Katherine Paterson has won two Newbery Medals, two National Book Awards and many other "best" book awards since 1977. She is known for writing from her heart, sharing her deepest feelings with words that will shape children's minds, and make us see and understand things we did not know before.

Reprinted with permission.
Illustration from *Bridge to Terabithia* by Katherine Paterson.
Illustrated by Donna Diamond. Copyright © 1977. Published by Thomas Y. Crowell.

BEATRIX POTTER

*"ONCE **upon a time there were four little rabbits, and their names were. . .***
Flopsy,
Mopsy,
Cotton-tail,
and Peter."

So begins the most famous picture letter ever written to a child. When five year old Noel Moore became ill, Beatrix Potter who was a friend of the family, sent him a letter about Peter Rabbit and his adventures in Mr. McGregor's garden. A few years later she asked Noel if she could borrow the letter to make a little book of the story. Luckily, he had kept it and so begins the tale of Beatrix Potter's career as an author and illustrator of some of the most admired and loved children's books ever written.

After receiving Noel's copy of her Peter Rabbit picture letter she rewrote the story, adding many more pen and ink drawings to the original version. She then tried to interest several book publishers in it but no one wanted such a *"little"* book. Big books for children were popular then but Beatrix Potter believed that her story should be able to fit into a child's hand and she did not want to change the size of her book or the illustrations. She decided to have it printed privately paying for the publishing herself. In 1901 the first privately printed edition of *Peter Rabbit* was published. She had ordered only 250 copies and they proved to be such a success that she ordered 200 more. Shortly thereafter, the Frederick Warne Company decided that they wanted to publish *Peter Rabbit* and they remained her publishers for the rest of her writing career.

Beatrix Potter was born in 1866 to wealthy parents who lived in London, England. There were many servants, nurses, and governesses who took care of Beatrix and her brother, Bertram. It was not customary for parents to play, read or eat with their children in those times and Beatrix had a lonely childhood. Her brother was sent away to boarding school but Beatrix was educated at home. When she was eight she began a sketchbook which she kept in secret code. She and her brother were allowed to keep pets in their upstairs nursery. . . rabbits, mice, frogs, salamanders, bats, squirrels. . . and she learned to draw them in great detail. Her own pet rabbit was called Peter.

She and her family would go on three month long vacations to Scotland every summer and there she would happily spend her days drawing and studying the plants and wild creatures around her.

Beatrix Potter was a very shy and quiet person all her life. She loved children and would write long illustrated story letters to cousins and other child friends. She also designed her own greeting cards for them. People say that she smiled frequently and had pretty blue eyes and a quiet, soft voice. When she would visit Noel Moore's family she would bring cages of white mice along to show them, opening the cage doors to let the mice run around the floor. No one seemed to mind!

Peter Rabbit was a financial success and Beatrix Potter was encouraged to write more *"little"* books. During the next ten years she wrote and illustrated a total of twenty-three. With the money she earned she bought Hill Top Farm at Sawrey in the Lake District of England. Farms and scenery from this area inspired many of her illustrations. People who visit Hill Top Farm today like to walk around the buildings and grounds trying to identify those that appeared in the *"little"* books.

Beatrix Potter's strict parents did not approve of her career as a writer or her business dealings. While living and working at Hill Top she met William Heelis, a lawyer who was helping her acquire more and more Lake District properties. They became engaged and later married even though her parents did not approve. Beatrix Potter was forty-seven years old by then and she wanted to live a simple life as a farmer's wife instead of the life her parents had chosen for her. Her marriage was a very happy one.

Beatrix Potter was interested in raising Herdwick sheep and she became quite an expert on them. She liked to talk about her sheep rather than her books when visitors came to call at Hill Top Farm. She also spent a great deal of time working to preserve the beautiful Lake District land from commercial development. She worked with an organization called the National Trust to keep the land the way it was. Beatrix bought more than 4,000 acres with her own money, giving them back to the National Trust as a park area. Her own home, Hill Top Farm, also was given to the National Trust after her death.

Although she never had any children, once she married she found little time for writing. However, some of her American friends urged her to continue to publish and she wrote *The Fairy Caravan* and a few other stories in her later years but they were not as successful as her earlier books.

Beatrix Potter lived to be seventy-seven years old, dying at her beloved Hill Top Farm on December 22, 1943. Her farm is preserved exactly as it was while she lived there for the thousands of fans who visit every year. Most of her watercolor paintings and drawings are kept in the Victoria and Albert Museum in London.

Her art work has influenced many other illustrators and delighted children and adults for almost ninety years. Several authors have used her illustrations to create books of their own. There are Beatrix Potter and Peter Rabbit painting books, knitting books, cookbooks, gardening books, counting books, bath books, story tapes, videos, calendars, ABC and puzzle books, pop-ups, cut-outs and stick books, and even a Peter Rabbit Diary. You can buy Beatrix Potter stuffed toys, porcelain figurines, puzzles, wall paper, jewelry, bed linens, games, dishes, and ornaments. We have a mania for Peter Rabbit!

Imagine how Beatrix Potter would feel if she could walk into a toy shop or book store today! She would see Peter and her other book characters represented in ways that are far different from the *"little"* books she created. I think she would be very pleased to know that she is still a very famous children's author and that a naughty rabbit wearing a blue jacket is instantly recognized by the name she gave him so many years ago.

Selected Books By Beatrix Potter

The Tale of Peter Rabbit
The Tale of Squirrel Nutkin
The Tailor of Gloucester
The Tale of Benjamin Bunny
The Tale of Two Bad Mice
The Tale of Mrs. Tiggy-Winkle
The Tale of Jeremy Fisher
The Tale of Tom Kitten
The Tale of Jemima Puddle-Duck
The Tale of the Flopsy Bunnies
The Tale of Mrs. Tittlemouse

The Tale of Timmy Tiptoes
The Tale of Johnny Town-Mouse
The Tale of Mr. Tod
The Tale of Pigling Bland
The Tale of the Pie and the Patty Pan
The Tale of Ginger and the Pickles
The Tale of Little Pig Robinson
The Story of the Fierce Bad Rabbit
The Story of Miss Moppet
Appley Dapply's Nursery Rhymes
Cecily Parsley's Nursery Rhymes

The Tale of Samuel Whiskers: Or, The Roly-Poly Pudding

TM

JACK PRELUTSKY

Jack Prelutsky collects miniature frogs *(non-living)*, writes funny poems, sings songs, plays the guitar, cooks, collects children's poetry books, plays sports, and likes to sit in his recliner chair. He also travels around the country talking to children, librarians, and teachers, answers lots of mail, creates collages and plastic sculpture, and finds time to write poems and stories for children. *Baby Ben (The Wild Baby), The Terrible Tiger, The Headless Horseman,* and *The New Kid on the Block* are all his creations.

This writer grew up in a section of New York City called the Bronx where people lived in apartment houses and everyone knew everyone else just like in a small town. The kids played games in the street and there wasn't a lot of crime or vandalism . Some of the things that happened to him in the Bronx turned up later in a book. When he talked about eating a worm or being tied to a tree in *Rolling Harvey Down the Hill* , he is remembering things that happened to him in real life.

Jack Prelutsky hated liver, beets, and poetry when he was a child. His mother made him eat liver once a week because she felt it was good for him. He would think of various ways of getting rid of it such as throwing it out the window, hiding it in the bed, etc. Like the liver, poetry was forced on Jack once a week by his elementary school teacher. None of the kids liked the poetry that this teacher said ***"was good for us."*** Jack suspected that the teacher didn't like it either. In those days he thought poets were sissy, boring, or dead; Something he assures us he is not! Jack Prelutsky's poems are full of humor, nonsense, and exaggeration. They deal with topics that kids really care about.

Jack was not interested in school and found it boring. However, he had a very fine singing voice and was paid to sing at weddings and other events when he was only ten years old. Later he was accepted at a special high school in New York City for very talented teenagers and was given free voice lessons by the Chorusmaster at the Metropolitan Opera. To this day he loves to sing and wishes that he could sing as well as the great opera star Luciano Pavarotti.

He became a poet almost accidentally. When he was twenty-four and thinking about being an artist he prepared two dozen animal sketches and wrote short poems to accompany them. A friend suggested that he show them to a publisher. The first publisher said, *"No thanks,"* but the second said, *"We'd like to publish your poems but without the art." "You have a natural talent for writing children's poetry."* That encouragement made him want to be a writer. Before that he had worked as a cabdriver, actor, furniture mover, folksinger, artist, photographer, potter, and store clerk among other things. He has always been a person with many different interests, hobbies and jobs.

Jack Prelutsky is married to a former librarian and they live in Albuquerque, New Mexico. As often as he can, he loves to go to their little cabin in the mountains where it is cool and he can look out at the tree-covered hills from his porch. The Prelutsky's have a pet Cairn Terrier named Fuzzy. His studio is a room in his house that contains a large writing desk, a computer, his library of children's books, his frog collection, and, of course, his recliner chair. He tries to write every day that he is home unless he gets involved with some other project around the house.

His parents taught him to read and he was reading by the time he was three years old. He can't remember not reading and loved it from the first moment he learned the alphabet. He loved *The Wind in the Willows* by Kenneth Grahame when he was a child and the *Grimm Fairy Tales* that his grandmother read to him during the summer nights he stayed with her.

When asked about some of his *"favorite"* things, he replied that questions about favorites were hard to answer but that he would do his best. His favorite sport is baseball and his favorite sport to play is racquetball. His favorite book is *The New Kid on the Block* although usually his favorite book is the one he is working on . His favorite memories are seeing his first book in print and seeing the Rocky Mountains for the first time from an airplane. His favorite foods seem to start with *"ch"*. . . cherries, cheese, chocolate, chimichangas, chips, chicken, and chocolate chip cookies! What he likes most about children is their honesty and what he likes least is their ability to ask questions that he can't answer. If he could have three wishes he would love to sing like Pavarotti, paint like Picasso, and dance like Fred Astaire.

Jack Prelutsky. . .

If **we** could have three wishes we wish you would write more, and MORE, and STILL MORE books for us!

Selected Books By Jack Prelutsky

The Baby Uggs are Hatching
It's Christmas
It's Halloween
It's Thanksgiving
It's Valentines Day
It's Snowing! It's Snowing!
The Mean Old Mean Hyena
My Parents Think I'm Sleeping
The New Kid on the Block
Nightmares: Poems to Trouble Your Sleep
The Headless Horseman Rides Tonight
The Queen of Eene
Rainy Rainy Saturday
Ride a Purple Pelican
Rolling Harvey Down the Hill
The Sheriff of Rottenshot
The Snopp of the Sidewalk and Other Poems
What I Did Last Summer
Brave Little Pete of Geranium Street
The Wild Baby
The Wild Baby Goes to Sea
The Wild Baby Gets a Puppy
Zoo Doings: Animal Poems
Tyrannosaurus Was A Beast

RICHARD SCARRY

Scarry rhymes with *"carry"* but don't plan on carrying all of Richard Scarry's books home from the library by yourself because he has written almost two hundred of them! They come in all sizes; big ones, small ones, activity books, picture paper-backs, and a series called the *Best Little Books Ever.* Each page in the Scarry books is filled with illustrations. This is done deliberately because he believes that kids love detail and lots of action and love to discover new things they haven't seen before. *"That's why I try to put as many things as I can on a page,"* he says. *"Nothing delights me more than to see a child reading a well-worn copy of one of my books held together with scotch tape. That's the way a book should look. . . used and enjoyed."*

Richard Scarry was born in Boston in 1919 and knew at a very young age that he wanted to draw. He went to the Boston Museum School of Fine Arts instead of a traditional college. He was in the Army during World War Two and afterwards moved to New York where he worked as a free-lance illustrator for magazines and book publishers doing work on stories written by others. He did this for eleven years before deciding to try writing and illustrating a book on his own. He took his idea for *The Best Word Book Ever* to a publisher called Golden Press and they liked it. In 1963 it was published and quickly became a best seller.

That was only the beginning of his successful career as an author and illustrator. Today over sixty million copies of his books have been sold in twenty-eight different languages.

Richard Scarry married a writer named Patricia *(Patsy)* Murphy and they had a son Richard *(always called Huck)* who is also an artist and author. Do you remember seeing the names Huck and Patsy in any of the Scarry books? They are there. Huck Scarry is grown-up now and has his own child. All the Scarry's live in Switzerland. They moved there because they love to ski. They love to travel and Richard and Patsy spend summers in France and also return to America several times each year. Patsy writes children's books, too, but cannot draw. The Scarry's tried working on books together but found that it was better to work apart on separate projects.

Richard Scarry believes that it is important to keep a regular work schedule and he goes to his studio every day. Dressed in a business suit, wearing sneakers, and carrying his lunch in a briefcase, this tall, gray-haired man takes the subway to his studio office in downtown Lausanne every morning at eight o'clock. He works there alone until four in the afternoon when he goes home to have tea with his family. He says, *"I am happiest when I'm working and I work even when I'm on vacation, making sketches of funny things I see."* His family and his work are his greatest pleasures.

This author illustrator wants his books to be both entertaining and educational. He feels that books are a better way of teaching children than television because they can be read again and again. He wants to be sure that his drawings and words are accurate. Before beginning a new book he does a great deal of research by reading. He knows that if he makes a mistake his readers will be quick to tell him about it.

Children all over the world love the Richard Scarry books. Hundreds of fan letters arrive daily at his home in Switzerland. His readers think that he must be the *"Best Writer Ever!"*

Selected Books By Richard Scarry

The Early Bird
Richard Scarry's What Do People Do All Day
Richard Scarry's Great Big Schoolhouse
Richard Scarry's ABC Word Book
Richard Scarry's Great Big Air Book
Richard Scarry's Best Counting Book Ever
Richard Scarry's Busiest People Ever
Early Words
Richard Scarry's Color Book
Richard Scarry's Lowly Worm Sniffy Book
Richard Scarry's Huckle's Book
Richard Scarry's Mix or Match Storybook
Richard Scarry's Best First Book Ever
Richard Scarry's Busytown Pop-Up Book
Richard Scarry's Lowly Worm Word Book
Richard Scarry's Funniest Storybook Ever
Richard Scarry's Great Big Mystery Book

Richard Scarry's Peasant Pig and the Terrible Dragon
Richard Scarry's Best Rainy Day Book Ever
Richard Scarry's Best Make-It Book Ever
Richard Scarry's Stories to Color
Richard Scarry's Toy Book
Richard Scarry's Find Your ABC's
Richard Scarry's Please and Thank You Book
Richard Scarry's Great Steamboat Mystery
Richard Scarry's Postman Pig and His Busy Neighbors
Busy Town, Busy People
Little ABC
Little Bedtime Book
Little Counting Book
Little Word Book
Mr. Fixit and Other Stories
Storytime
Things to Learn

WILLIAM STEIG

William Steig, author and illustrator, was born in 1907 into a family of artists. He attended New York City public schools and then went to City College. After that he studied at the National Academy of Design.

He began his career as a cartoonist. When he was 23 years old, his first work appeared in *The New Yorker* magazine. For almost forty years he continued as a successful cartoonist.

In 1968 his career took a surprising turn when he published his first children's book. It was a book of cartoons, but there were no words under the drawings, just letters. But if you read the letters out loud, they sound like words. If you say the letters *"C D B"* out loud, it sounds like the words *"see the bee."* *"I I Q"* becomes *"I like you."* The book is lots of fun! Many years later, William Steig published another book like this one called *C D C?* Can you guess what it's about?

Cartooning, he says, is much different from writing books. When you are a cartoonist, you work alone and sketch the ideas for cartoons when they come to you. You send them in the mail to the magazine. If they like the cartoon, they send you a check and publish it; if they don't like it they return it to you. And you hardly ever hear from the people who see your cartoon and enjoy it.

Writing and illustrating books is a whole different kettle of fish. It takes more time, more space, and more work. With cartoons, they can all be different; in a book all the pictures have to fit together and look just right.

Once he decides it's time to work on a new book, he works it in different ways. Sometimes a beginning picture will give him the idea for the whole rest of the book. That's how he created *Roland the Minstrel Pig.* Other times a picture comes into his head, But it's not at the beginning of the story... it fits in more towards the end. That's how *Amos and Boris* worked out. Still other times he decides first what the whole book will be about and then goes on from there. That's how *Sylvester and the Magic Pebble* and *Dominic* came about.

While he's working he never really plans everything out beforehand or sticks to it no matter what. *"I just ramble around and discover for myself what will happen next."*

If readers are surprised by what happens in his stories, imagine how surprised William Steig is when he dreams them up! Maybe as surprised as Solomon the rabbit in *Solomon the Rusty Nail* the first time he scratches his nose and wiggles his tail at the same time. Read it and find out what happens. Or maybe as surprised as Sylvester is when he finds the Magic Pebble.

William Steig makes up stories and he sometimes makes up words. Ordinary thunder *"crashes"* or *"booms."* Not in *Farmer Palmer's Wagon Ride.* That stormy thunder *"dramberamberooms"* and *"Bombombs!"* Now **that's** thunder.

After all his years working as a cartoonist and hardly ever hearing from his fans, Mr. Steig enjoys being famous and receiving loads of fan mail from his admiring readers.

Book writing will never be lonely for William Steig.

Selected Books By William Steig

C D B!	Abel's Island
Roland the Minstrel Pig	The Amazing Bone
Sylvester and the Magic Pebble	Caleb & Kate
The Bad Island	C D C?
Bad Speller	The Zabajaba Jungle
Eye for Elephants	Brave Irene
Lovely Ones	Solomon the Rusty Nail
Male/Female	Doctor De Soto
Amos and Boris	Gorky Rises
Dominic	Spinky Sulks
The Real Thief	Tiffky Doofky
Farmer Palmer's Wagon Ride	Yellow and Pink

Reprinted with permission.
Illustration from *Sylvester and the Magic Pebble* by William Steig.
Copyright © 1969 by William Steig.
Published by Simon & Schuster.

GERTRUDE CHANDLER WARNER

Gertrude Chandler Warner waited forty years for a wish to come true. But for her, it was well worth the wait. Read on to find out what that special wish was and how it came true.

Gertrude was one of two daughters born to Edgar and Jane Warner. Young Gertrude loved the outdoors. She collected moths and butterflies, she collected and pressed wild flowers, and she learned to recognize all the different kinds of birds by sight and sound. For thirty-two years Gertrude taught in the elementary school in Putnam, Connecticut where she was born and raised. She always wanted to be a writer, but her mother had told Gertrude and her sister that they'd better find real jobs because they would never make any money writing.

When she was growing up, Gertrude's house was across from a railroad. She and her friends would often sit by the tracks for hours at a time watching the trains go by. Her favorite railroad car was the caboose. Sometimes when the train stopped she could look through the window of the caboose and see what was inside: a small coal-burning stove, a little table, coffee cups with no saucers, and a tin coffee pot sitting on the stove. She often dreamed about what it would be like to live in a caboose and ride the rails on different adventures. Many years later, these dreams and memories from her childhood would help her create her best-loved stories.

Gertrude once said, *"I am telling the exact truth when I say that my sister and I began to write when we were just able to hold a pencil."* And to keep the two little girls from writing on countless little bits of paper and leaving them all over the house, their mother would buy them each a little ten-cent blank book to keep their words, sentences, and stories in. *(This is something you might enjoy doing.)* The first book she remembers making as a child was a book which she also illustrated with watercolors. She presented this book to her beloved grandfather. She made it a practice to give him a handmade book every Christmas after that. Her grandfather was her first audience.

Gertrude had a very bad case of bronchitis and could not go to school. She had already written eight books on special order for a religious organization. This time she decided that she would write a book that she wanted to write. *"What would I like to* do?" she asked herself. *"Well, I would like to live in a freight car, or a caboose. I would hang my wash out on the little back piazza and cook my stew on the little rusty stove found in the caboose."* Read the Boxcar books and see if that's what she wrote about.

Now this is where her forty-year-old wish comes true.

After she had already written so many successful Boxcar children's books. . . there are nineteen in all. . .she became curious about modern cabooses and how they compared to the old fashioned kind she saw as a youngster. She became so curious that she wrote a letter to a friend of hers who was a retired railroad engineer. Her friend, Mr. Donovan, called her on the telephone and told her that the cabooses were not different and that if she would like to find out for herself, he would be happy to arrange to take her on a tour of one.

"When the great day came," she said, *"off we went to the freight yard. And there, right by the freight-platform, was a caboose. How exciting it was to step inside at last! There just as I remembered, was a little stove(although not coal-burning), the cups with no saucers, and all the rest."*

Gertrude Chandler Warner still thought it would be wonderful to live in a caboose. And she felt, too, that actually going inside a real caboose was a wish come true. A forty-year-old wish that was well worth the wait.

Selected Books by Gertrude Chandler Warner

The House of Delight	Houseboat Mystery
Star Stories	Lighthouse Mystery
The World in a Barn	Mike's Mystery
Windows into Alaska	Mountain Top Mystery
The World on a Farm	Mystery Behind the Wall
Children of the Harvest	Mystery in the Sand
Benny Uncovers a Mystery	Mystery Ranch
Bicycle Mystery	Schoolhouse Mystery
Blue Bay Mystery	Snowbound Mystery
Boxcar Children	Surprise Island
Bus Station Mystery	Tree House Mystery
Caboose Mystery	Woodshed Mystery
	Yellow House Mystery